THE
DUMPLING
FIELD

THE
DUMPLING
FIELD

Haiku of Issa

Translated by Lucien Stryk

with the assistance of Noboru Fujiwara

Swallow Press Ohio University Press
Athens

Swallow Press/Ohio University Press books are printed on acid-free paper ∞

Library of Congress Cataloging-in-Publication Data

Kobayashi, Issa, 1763–1827.
  [Poems. English]
  The dumpling field : haiku of Issa / translated by Lucien Stryk, with the
assistance of Noboru Fujiwara.
    p.   cm.
  ISBN 0-8040-0952-X. — ISBN 0-8040-0953-8 (pbk.)
  1. Kobayashi, Issa, 1763–1827—Translations into English.
2. Haiku—Translations into English.   I. Stryk, Lucien.
II. Fujiwara, Noboru, 1916–1989.   III. Title.
PL797.2.A25   1991b
895.6'134—dc20   91-17639
                                                         CIP
03 02 01 00 99 98   7 6 5 4 3

To the Memory of
Noboru Fujiwara
and for Theo,
of Issa's loyal company

NOTE

For permission to use material included thanks are due the editors and publishers of *American Poetry Review, Colorado-North Review, London Magazine, Mid-American Review, The Penguin Book of Zen Poetry* (Swallow Press/Ohio University Press and Penguin Books Ltd., 1977), and *Of Pen and Ink and Paper Scraps* (Swallow Press/Ohio University Press, 1989).

The world? Moonlit
drops shaken
from the crane's bill.
DOGEN

INTRODUCTION

1

I stroll by the Open Air Theater in Regent's Park, London, and sit on a bench nearby to catch the poetry of *A Midsummer Night's Dream* this hazy midsummer evening, in walking distance of the spot where Shakespeare's company first spoke these lines. It sounds as if the first scene of act 4 has now begun, and I imagine Titania's entrance with her attendants, Peas-blossom, Cobweb, Moth, Mustard-seed, and all the other fairies. Droll Bottom, now an ass, coaxes one fairy to scratch his head, another to fetch a "red-hipp'd humble bee on the top of a thistle, and . . . the honey-bag." In Ass's Eden, Bottom, loved by all, loves all in return. Soon will come his rude awakening; restored to human shape he will have little in common with fays and fairy queens.

Suddenly I am aware of a companion. One of London's countless ragged wanderers sits happily beside me. He opens one of several bags, takes out a sandwich and, after a few chomps, begins sharing his fare with the gathering birds and a gray-tail squirrel. He chuckles as they frisk for scraps, and says he could now do with a good cup of tea. "Swig it morning, noon and night," he says, "while the rest of 'em swig from the bottle. Call me "Cuppa tea," they do—it's a fact." Off he goes, leaving me to the creatures still coveting traces of bread, and I'm caught up again in the sounds of the play.

Two hundred years after Shakespeare first enchanted London with the wonder and sympathy of his dream, another poet thousands of miles away was wetting his ink-stone and brushing poem on poem with wonder and sympathy for the world of creatures large and small, loved and despised:

> Watch out,
> young sparrows—
> Prince Horse trots close.

Children,
don't harm the fleas,
with children.

Silverfish escaping—
mothers,
fathers, children.

Among the four greatest haiku poets of Japan, Issa (1763–1827) differs from the others, Basho (1644–1694), Buson (1715–1783), and Shiki (1867–1902) in many ways. Perhaps what most distinguishes him are his tenderness and compassion. Issa is best read in a well-trodden backyard, midsummer, filled with flies, fireflies, wasps, mosquitoes *and* peas-blossoms, cobwebs, moths, and mustard-seeds. For it is here, with birds, cats, rabbits, dogs and squirrels nearby, he is most himself.

Issa is necessary to us because his values, which must become ours if we are to survive as humans, are those most severely threatened in our world. At a moment when summer-evening creatures are blasted with insect "zappers" and dizzied with the stench of poison, he reminds us, over and over, of the individual reality of each life destroyed. Yet— and it is this which gives his poems pathos—he is not above swatting a fly or mosquito, caught up in the small personal drama of survival. But at how great a cost! Some of his best pieces are elegies for creatures wantonly killed, some by himself:

Each time I swat
a fly, I squint
at the mountain.

First cicada:
life is
cruel, cruel, cruel.

2

Though he was as keen a traveler as his favorite Basho, forever the itinerant poet, in Issa's case journeys were undertaken because home was in the cruelest sense denied him. His birthplace, to which he was passionately attached, was the source of his finest lines. Like Basho and others he tried to establish himself in Edo (now Tokyo), but he was for the most part uneasy there, always at heart the country boy, his imagination kindled by nature.

Yataro Kobayashi, who took the pen-name Issa (Cup of Tea), was the first son of a farmer of Kashiwabara in the province of Shinano (now Nagano Prefecture). He was educated chiefly by a village teacher who wrote haiku under the pen-name Shimpo, exposing him at a very early age to the art. His mother died when he was three, and five years later his father remarried. The stepmother was insensitive to the child, and in 1777 he left home for Tokyo to find work, often forced to do most menial jobs. By 1787 he was studying haiku with Chikua, a poet of the Basho-inspired Katsushika group, and he began to distinguish himself. Following Chikua's death in 1790, he decided —very much in emulation of Basho—to live as a poet, and spent the next ten years journeying.

He visited fellow writers on his way, exchanging ideas on the art of haiku. On occasion he brought out a collection of his verse. In 1801, when his father died, he wrote *Diary of My Father's Death*. His father's wish was that he should settle in the old home in Kashiwabara, but problems with his stepmother and half-brother, who lived there, made this impossible, and he was unable to move back until 1813. In 1814 he married a woman named Kiku, and they had four children in quick succession. None survived. The birth and death of the second of these, his daughter Sato, inspired him to write *Spring of My Life* (1819), perhaps his best-known work: a *haibun* (haiku mixed with prose), it is an account of what was to him his most important year. He continued writing haiku, but his last years were saddened by the death of Kiku in 1823.

He married again in 1824, but was soon divorced. In 1827, his house burnt down, and in poverty and heartbroken, he died, survived by a third wife and unborn child.

In a life of countless misfortunes, perhaps the greatest was that as unwanted stepson after his beloved father's death, Issa was denied a place in his family home, which embittered his life for many years. Then the death of his children, one after the other, devastated his spirit. Things which other perhaps less emotional men might have taken in stride, he could not overcome, and in poem after poem we find him succumbing:

> Outliving
> them all, all—
> how cold.

How he must have envied Basho's Zen detachment, Buson's unruffled striving for perfection. There is nothing heroic about Issa, his art is never cold: to live, he discovered, is to suffer, to be poet is to record that suffering. Some who go to art for lives larger than their own may think Issa's poetry soft, sentimental, but one thing he can do better than anyone is stir us with the knowledge that a painful, impoverished life can have moments of generous warmth, even gaiety:

> I'm leaving—
> now you can make love,
> my flies.

3

Issa's output, when compared with others, was prodigious. He wrote scores of haiku, many more than Basho. Indeed he wrote compulsively, and those who have no taste for casual insights might think some pieces less than poems:

One bath
after another —
how stupid.

Yet who would wish him silent at such moments, contrasting
the ordinary so sharply with the profound:

Where there are humans
you'll find flies,
and Buddhas.

And would a man's spirit be fully expressed if only the depths
were revealed? He could not help the ever-rising lightness
above misery, could not resist poking fun, chiefly at himself.

Issa was always ready to acknowledge a debt to Basho, and
although like him he was to have disciples, he advised them
not to follow his practice but emulate the master. He was at
all times conscious of the difference between Basho and
himself: Issa's art, never exalted, is bold in its use of common
idiom and filled with ordinary details of everyday life. There
is ever-present wit and constant personification, and though
he clowns the laughter is never cruel. The poverty of his life,
its many traumas, all with their sharp effect, led him to sym-
pathize with all, neighbor and insect. He was after all a Shin-
shu Buddhist, and like all the sect's practitioners took seriously
the doctrine's faith in the sacredness of life, as expressed in the
Vinaya-pitaka section of the *Tripitaka*, the Bible of Buddhism.

How can you, foolish men, dig the ground . . . ?
There are living things in the ground. How can you,
foolish men, fell a tree? There are living things in
the tree. Whatever man should intentionally deprive
a breathing thing of life, there is an offence of
expiation.

4

Haiku structure had become by Issa's time a profound ortho-doxy: seventeen syllables arranged precisely 5-7-5, two elements divided by a break (*kireji* — cutting word — which in English is best rendered by punctuation): the first element, the object, condition or situation; the second, preceded by *kireji*, the vital perception. The desired effect was, and has remained, a moment in its crystallized state, a distillation of impressions, including seasonal, all related to transcendent unity. There is little doubt, therefore, that the poet is encour-aged to seek totality of experience. Haiku is meant to snare life's keenest visions, one after another, high and low, fair and foul, strong and weak, manifesting the importance of each, taking care *not* to choose the "poetic" while at the same time valuing it.

Issa gives us perhaps the largest, most varied gamut of ex-perience amongst all his fellow artists, not because he lived more or was a greater hand with words, but because he had the deepest need to clarify for himself the meaning of all that could be seen and felt. Although he did not train, as Basho did, under a Zen master, Buddhist he was, and as one of the elder poet's most devoted admirers, he could not help bring-ing to his work those attitudes unique to Zen. Indeed Basho, as modern haiku's virtual creator, assured the predominance in this art of the principles and aesthetic long associated with the ancient sect.

What are these principles and what is that aesthetic, as found in the poems of one not Zennist but living in a world perme-ated by its ideals? And, of equal importance, what have all works of art touched by Zen in common? What distinguishes them from works their equal yet not related? Here is the Rinzai Zen master Tenzan Yasuda's reply to just such questions, asked some years ago at his temple, the Joeiji, in Yamaguchi:

> What expresses cosmic truth in the most direct and
> concise way — that is the heart of Zen art. Please

examine this picture ("Fisherman and Woodcutter" by Sesshu): of all the artist's pictures, this is my favorite. The boat at the fisherman's back tells us his occupation, the bundle of firewood behind the woodcutter tells his. The fisherman is drawn with only three strokes of the brush, the woodcutter with five. You couldn't ask for greater concision. And these two men, what are they talking about? In all probability, and this the atmosphere of the picture suggests, they are discussing something very important, something beneath the surface of daily life. How do I know? Why, every one of Sesshu's brush strokes tells me . . . . Western art has volume and richness when it is good. Yet to me it is too thickly encumbered by what is dispensable. It's as if the Western artist were trying to hide something, not reveal it.

Leaving aside the provocative conclusion of the master's comment, we are struck first by the high place given concision as aesthetic ideal—for Zennist, less is *truly* more. What becomes evident at once, and is most significant, is the desirability of participation in the work, the viewer's or reader's active penetration into the creative process. Suggestion, so essential to all arts associated with Zen, is central to haiku. Why this should be is hard to explain, but poems most appreciated are those proving most personal to the reader, a crumb of life discovered suddenly. Here is a piece by Boncho, who died fifty years before Issa's birth:

Nightingale—
my clogs
stick in the mud.

That the poet, transfixed by bird-song, is deeply sensitive would be apparent to all practiced readers. One extra word would have spoiled the impression, proved intolerable. The poem which most fully invites involvement, all else equal, is bound to be most admired. Here is Basho:

Summer grasses,
all that remains
of soldiers' dreams.

Here Buson:

A sudden chill—
in our room my dead wife's
comb, underfoot.

And here Shiki:

Autumn wind:
gods, Buddha—
lies, lies, lies.

5

Perhaps responsible for the five centuries of haiku has been
its capacity to inspire such very different sensibilities. Its first
practitioners, Sogi (1421–1502), Sokan (1458–1546), and Mori-
take (1472–1549) had the task of establishing as legitimate form
an element drawn from the reigning *tanka*, which was strictly
structured as a pattern of 5–7–5–7–7 syllables. Along with the
choka and *sedoka*, the *tanka* was prominent in the earliest col-
lection of Japanese poetry, the eighth century *Manyoshu*. It must
have taken daring of a sort, in a society so rule-bound, to break
up ancient forms in hope of revitalization. If the haiku of its
first makers, important as it was, had little appeal to Basho
and his successors, they always spoke gratefully of it. From
the very start, largely due to Basho, haiku at its best was seen
as revelatory, possessing qualities in common with other arts
based on an essentially Zen aesthetic: simplicity, directness,
naturalness, profundity. And each poem had its dominant

mood, one of four subtly categorized: *sabi* (isolation), *wabi* (poverty), *aware* (impermanence), *yugen* (mystery). To haiku's finest artists its brevity was seen less as barrier than challenge to the imagination, demanding that however broad in implication the poem would have to be of single impact.

For Zennists like Basho the haiku event was realized in a state of near meditation, similar to the monastic practice of mind-pointing. In the earliest stage of training the disciple might be asked to point the mind at various objects, continuing until it stops wandering, associating, metaphorizing — in short, wobbling. The mind penetrates the object ever more deeply, until one with it; the state of *muga*, as such identification is known in Zen, is attained. Little in Issa's background as Shinshu Buddhist would have led to such ambition, let alone effort, for his sect, most liberal of all, in making altruistic social contact among its most important goals would have been inclined to discourage the necessary solitariness and abstemiousness of Zen. But Issa's inspiration was Basho, and the great poet's comments on the art of life and poetry, faithfully recorded by disciples, were held sacred. Thus his adoption of Zen attitudes was natural. If through deep human bondage he found it impossible to live freely as the unattached Basho, he could nevertheless approach the events of life with the hope of memorializing the most important of them.

Though Issa is considered the simplest of haiku's famous four, he too is capable of reaching depths, and is honored as being closest to the common man, sharing in the everyday world all know and suffer. It is chiefly for that he is most loved. And yet there are those who appear to regard him as excessivly soft. Such a puzzling attitude is by no means uncommon in Japan, even among Zennists, whose view is based on a principle rooted in doctrine: the need to achieve and thereafter constantly to practice non-attachment, of the kind which might help overcome serious mental problems beyond the numerous small difficulties of existing. Among the stigma categorized are the "stepson mentality," and "poverty complex," both of which are said to have possessed him.

Often one so possessed is encouraged to seek guidance of a Zen master, and if in such context one compares Issa's life and work with that of others, one must concede that he might indeed have been helped. But would we, then, have the poems?

Those who care most for art, East or West, would wish the artist a happy, carefree life, but often the tensions of a life are the very source of uniqueness. If Issa remained attached fatally to things "unworthy," it is that which lay behind his overwhelming compassion, which was not limited to fellow humans. He was the poet of the ignored, the despised, and his eye—keen as his heart was large—was capable of the subtlest gradations:

> Don't kill the fly—
> it wrings its hands,
> its feet.

Such poems have had lasting impact on Japanese literature as a whole, and it is not surprising to find modern poets such as the Zennist Shinkichi Takahashi acknowledging a debt to Issa. Here is Takahashi at his compassionate best, in "Camel":

> The camel's humps
> shifted with clouds.
>
> Such solitude beheads!
> My arms stretch
>
> beyond mountain peaks,
> flame in the desert.

6

Issa's range, as we have seen, was unlimited and unconventional, yet in poetic form he was altogether a traditionalist, more so than Basho, who was known to depart on occasion from formal orthodoxy, even flaunting syllabic limitations. Indeed a contemporary haiku school, the Soun, offers Basho's example as justification for its practice of "free verse." Not only did Issa conform to established pattern, he took care to abide by all accepted norms of the art, including seasonal suggestion. As Basho's disciple he was aware of the well-nigh canonical stature given Basho's comments on haiku's desired qualities. Chief among these were use of colloquial language, symbolic expression leading to gravity of feeling, and above all else unity of tone. He seemed especially taken with Basho's elevation of the commonplace, ordinary things and events of everyday life. Anything could be lifted and refined, the lower the subject, the better.

Basho used highly suggestive terms to make points clear. Good poems possessed *karumi* (lightness of touch), *sabi* (dryness), *hosomi* (thinness), and with all that there had to be *shiori* (warmth of feeling). He was to state:

> You can learn about the pine only from the pine, about the bamboo only from the bamboo. Observing an object you must leave aside preoccupation with self, for if you do not, you impose yourself, hence do not learn from it. The object and you must become one, and from this oneness comes the poem.

Basho insisted on a highly conscious approach to composition, even to the extent of identifying essential elements, among them *utsuri* (color), *nioi* (smell), *hibiki* (tone) and *kurai* (grace). All, fused, were meant to assure harmony of feeling, without which there could not be true poetry. Throughout his life Issa listened to the master, and learned.

Basho's striving for poetic harmony is especially clear in his *haibun*, which match his verse in depth and imaginative flight. His *haibun* are essentially travel sketches, most having very suggestive titles: *The Records of a Weather-Exposed Skeleton* (1684–5), *A Visit to Kashima Shrine* (1687), *The Records of a Travel-Worn Satchel* (1688) and, best-known of all, *The Narrow Road to the Deep North* (1689). Marvels of organic structure, they have been emulated by many, matched by none.

In spite of its great interest, Issa's *haibun*, *Oraga Haru (Spring of My Life)*, is, apart from its haiku — among his finest — a simple record, throughout 1819, of daily toils and turmoils, as the following excerpt reveals:

> At the height of joy, comes sorrow — thus goes the world. Like a small pine tree which hardly had half the joy of a thousand years, our daughter Sato with her second leaf just out, full of laughter, was seized by the cruel god of smallpox . . . . For awhile she seemed to recover, then she grew weaker and weaker . . . until finally, on the twenty-first day of the sixth month, she left the world with the bloom of a morning-glory. Her mother clasped her face and sobbed — who would have blamed her. But the child's time had come . . . the flowing water would not return, the fallen blossom would not return to its branch. We tried to resign ourselves . . . but could not stop thinking of her, our love was so strong.

> World of dew?
> Perhaps,
> and yet . . .

The poet's venture into *haibun* was surely important, and *Spring of My Life* does precisely what he had hoped, shoring up events that meant most to him. Though somewhat sketchy, the work adds greatly to his output. His *haibun*, as well as his poems, details his life moment by moment, giving a full day-to-day sense of his humanity. And if compared with his more austere company he sometimes, as result of intense attachments, loses control, we love him all the more.

7

Darkness has fallen over the bench where I sit. Words from the stage no longer drift my way. Actors and audience have left to Puck's soft words, which will follow into their sleep:

> If we shadows have offended,
> Think but this, and all is mended, —
> That you have but slumbered here . . . .

Now the creatures, in the spirit of the night, reclaim their world. Somewhere far away, in time and space, a poet needs a friend:

> First firefly,
> why turn away—
> it's Issa.

THE POEMS

SPRING

1

Cherry blossoms?
In these parts
grass also blooms.

2

Owls are calling,
"Come, come,"
to the fireflies.

3

Listen,
all creeping things —
the bell of transience.

4

Don't weep, insects —
lovers, stars themselves,
must part.

5

Cuckoo sings
to me, to the mountain,
in turn.

6

Flies swarming —
what do they want of
these wrinkled hands?

7

Where there are humans
you'll find flies,
and Buddhas.

8

Farmer,
pointing the way
with a radish.

9

Short night —
scarlet flower
at vine's tip.

10

Buddha's Nirvana,
beyond flowers,
and money.

11

When plum
blooms —
a freeze in hell.

12

What a world,
where lotus flowers
are ploughed into a field.

13

Passing without
a glance —
first firefly.

14

I'm leaving —
now you can make love,
my flies.

15

Nightingale's song
this morning,
soaked with rain.

16

Children,
don't harm the flea,
with children.

17

Borrowing my house
from insects,
I slept.

18

Watch it — you'll bump
your heads
on that stone, fireflies.

19

From the bough
floating down river,
insect song.

20

First firefly,
why turn away —
it's Issa.

21

Under cherry trees
there are
no strangers.

22

Mokuboji Temple —
fireflies come even
to the barking dog.

23

In my house
mice and fireflies
get along.

24

Treated shabbily
by fleas, by flies,
day quits.

25

Reflected
in the dragonfly's eye —
mountains.

26

In spring rain
how they carry on,
uneaten ducks.

27

Vines tight
around scorched rocks —
midday glories.

28

Moist spring moon —
raise a finger
and it drips.

29

House burnt down —
fleas
dance in embers.

30

Bound to a tree,
mischievous boy
bawls to a firefly.

31

Rice-field dawn —
would you were here,
my dead father.

32

Fuji dusk —
back to back,
frogs are chanting.

33

Sundown —
under cherry blooms
men scurry home.

34

Early spring —
stream flows
toward my door.

35

Whitebait,
darting
into dusk's haze.

36

Watch out,
young sparrows —
Prince Horse trots close.

37

Come, sparrow
orphan,
play with me.

38

Old pillar,
sized by
a spanworm.

39

Each time I swat
a fly, I squint
at the mountain.

40

Spring evening —
how bold the
horned owl's stare.

41

Playing stone,
frog lets
the horse sniff.

42

Kitten
on the scale,
plays on.

43

In my old place
flies
nettle anyone.

44

Don't kill the fly —
it wrings
its hands, its feet.

45

Weary cormorant—
scolded,
plunges once again.

46

Great moon
woven in plum scent,
all mine.

47

Cherry-petal confetti
showers my
muddy straw sandals.

48

Tonight's moon-viewing —
this slope
was high enough.

49

Song of skylark —
night falls
from my face.

50

Moment of
fierceness, in
the first butterfly.

51

After night in
the dog's bowl,
butterfly scoots off.

52

Cherry blossoms
everywhere: this
undeserving world.

53

Frog and I,
eyeball
to eyeball.

54

Opening my umbrella
in spring rain,
I dare Hakone Pass.

55

What bliss: spring
rain, watching
flames lick the pot.

56

Spring breeze —
lapping Sumida River,
wharf-rat.

57

Bamboo shoot,
springing up
just anywhere.

58

Reed warblers
sing the great river
still.

59

Tree meant for
the axe, yet birds
still build their nests.

60

Cherry time:
coop-birds, eyes shut,
sing together.

61

Plum in bloom —
the Gates of Hell
stay shut.

62

Wonderful —
under cherry blossoms,
this gift of life.

63

My empty face,
betrayed
by lightning.

64

Quavering shrike —
impatient
once again?

65

Lone girl in tree
shadow, hums
the rice-planting song.

66

Tormenting my
siesta — song
of rice-planters.

67

Again well met —
spring waters,
smoke-plume of Mount Asama.

68

Skylark —
flying down
for lunch.

69

Spring rain —
rat lapping
bamboo leaf.

70

Young leaves,
splashing
the white wall.

71

Silk-worm spilling
a cocoon
in Buddha's lap.

72

Dodging the crowd,
grasping
a poppy.

73

Evening cherry blooms —
is today
really yesterday?

74

Flute practice for
the fête greens
the young rice-plants.

75

Imagine — cherries
still bloom round my
abandoned house.

76

Cuckoo song —
cherries of Shinano
bursting with flower.

77

Shower: caught in
lightning flash —
me, the death-hater.

78

Spring rain —
duck zig-zags
to the gate.

79

Woodpecker nosing
round the hut,
appraising.

80

Plum blossom branch —
moon urges me
to steal you.

81

Tomcat's falsetto,
luring
a tabby.

82

Traveler,
planting the stream-borne
rice-plant.

83

Plum scent —
guest won't mind
the chipped cup.

84

Field tilling —
babe crawls
through horsetails.

85

Earthworm pops up —
how quick
the ants.

86

Spring rain —
sparrows, open mouthed,
beak at my lunch.

87

Bush warbler —
nest beyond reach
of song.

88

Rustling
the grassy field —
departing spring.

SUMMER

89

Clouds of mosquitoes —
it would be bare
without them.

90

At prayer,
bead-swinging
at mosquitoes.

91

Skylarks singing —
the farmer
makes a pillow of his hoe.

92

Shush, cicada —
old Whiskers
is about.

93

From burweed,
such a butterfly
was born?

94

When I go,
guard my tomb well,
grasshopper.

95

A poor quarter:
flies, fleas, mosquitoes
live forever

96

From those swarming
clouds,
a shower of ants.

97

Cooling melon —
at a hint of footsteps,
you're a frog.

98

Cicada ji, ji, jiing —
my head, this house
are rock.

99

Grasshopper's song in
moonlight — someone's
survived the flood.

100

Bon festival —
child claps hands,
waking dead mother.

101

Field gambling —
grasshoppers
leaping coin to coin.

102

Red rice — from
the fox's lair,
heat waves.

103

Back gate opens
itself —
how long the day.

104

In and out
the long day,
folks in the parlor.

105

How red
the pinwheel,
cry the cicadas.

106

Heat waves —
his smile still
before me.

107

Plunging skylark —
heaven moved
by a boy's cry.

108

Summer shower —
naked horse,
naked rider.

109

Monk, fly,
mosquito,
pass me by!

110

How still — is this
the last fly
I will fan from him?

111

Weaving butterfly,
I am no more
than dust.

112

How joyous —
rebirth as butterflies
of the field.

113

How thrilled
you seem,
you tiger moth.

114

Fireworks
kindling the lake —
how brief.

115

Gleam of left-over
bean-curd —
mosquitoes buzz.

116

Through a chink
in the mosquito ranks,
the capital.

117

Somersaulting
through the flower-field,
our dog.

118

Such a moon —
even the turtle
tells the hour.

119

My girl's cheek
against melon-doll —
a dream.

120

Mosquitoes everywhere —
once more
an old man's world.

121

Morning glory —
whose face
is without fault?

122

Heaped oyster shells —
Fukagawa
aglow in moonlight.

123

How clear —
cicada over
sunset lake.

124

Puppy-eyed
morning-glories,
awake at the door.

125

Daybreak —
working as one,
two butterflies.

126

Snail — baring
shoulders
to the moon.

127

Heat waves —
cats worship
the God of Love.

128

Fireflies
entering my house,
don't despise it.

129

Into the house
before me,
fly on my hat.

130

Snail —
always
at home.

131

Rose of Sharon —
forgive me,
I must sleep.

132

Iris —
sharpened
by sun-beams.

133

Tipping the field
of rape-flowers —
Mount Fuji.

134

Road beckoning,
I snatch up
my fan.

135

The fan —
no sooner found
than lost.

136

Day's mosquito
over my shoulder —
stony silence.

137

Drenched
dragonfly —
what's to do?

138

Snail, finding
the path
to my foot.

139

Startled
by the frog —
my shadow.

140

Bush wasps, keep
your distance —
here, and beyond.

141

Two feet into
insect smudge —
moonlight.

142

Giant firefly,
how soft
your light.

143

Don't fret,
insects —
time will restore.

144

My old home —
Buddha face
of the snail.

145

Sadness of cool
melons — two days
nobody's come.

146

Garden kidnap —
butterfly slips off
with another.

147

Playtime — dragonfly
shimmies its tail
in Sumida River.

148

Old dog, stirred
by the hum
of earth-worms.

149

Soaking in the hot-spring,
I give butterfly
a break.

150

Summer mountain,
plumped
by moonlight.

151

Sunset through
the pine tree,
flowering eulalia grass.

152

Summer rain —
plant flowers
at the high window.

153

Giddying
the counter clerk —
drunken butterflies.

154

Summer — farmers
straw-beating,
chaffing the moonlight.

155

Dragonfly,
sizing up
Mount Fuji.

156

What a day —
larks soar to heaven,
men gather shells.

157

Summer field —
thunder,
or my empty stomach.

158

Suddenly
over deep grass,
swallows!

159

Where once the builder's
scythe laid waste,
there's rice full in the ear.

160

Out together —
bean-curd man,
noon-time glories.

161

Radishes pulled one
by one, while
sparrows trill for space.

162

Cool breeze,
tangled
in a grass-blade.

163

Short night: snoring
under trees, on rocks —
traveling priests.

164

Crescent moon,
enticing
new mosquitoes.

165

Water-bird, busy
going nowhere —
dusk to dusk.

166

Praying mantis —
one hand
on temple bell.

167

Cricket on
the palette —
painting a whisker.

168

Letting grasshopper
go, I'm repaid
with a nip!

169

Sardine season —
even the dog
will dine.

170

Field crow,
lost in
the banana tree.

171

Sparrows bathe
on lotus leaves —
not one drop left.

172

Cricket sails
downriver,
fifty feet or so.

173

After day's heat —
ah, cool water
on the horse's rump.

174

Pure midsummer sky,
not even a smudge
of cloud.

175

Singing skylark —
that narrow path
leads to the sea.

176

Lord Toad, your Lady
pines, your children
may be weeping.

177

Step by step
up summer mountain —
suddenly the sea.

AUTUMN

178

Autumn wind,
the beggar looks
me over, sizing up.

179

Buddha Law,
shining
in leaf dew.

180

A good world,
dew-drops fall
by ones, by twos.

181

Let's take
the duckweed way
to clouds.

182

First cicada:
life is
cruel, cruel, cruel.

183

Autumn evening —
knees in arms,
like a saint.

184

Don't fly off, nightingale —
though your song's poor,
you're mine.

185

Five yen each:
a cup of tea,
the nightingale.

186

Autumn wind —
mountain's shadow
wavers.

187

My hut,
thatched
with morning glories.

188

Never forget:
we walk on hell,
gazing at flowers.

189

In this world
even butterflies
must earn their keep.

190

As we grow old,
what triumph
burning mosquitoes.

191

Cuckoo's crying —
nothing special to do,
nor has the burweed.

192

Be respectful,
sparrow,
of our old bedding.

193

Dew spread,
the seeds of hell
are sown.

194

Cries of wild geese,
rumors
spread about me.

195

Geese, fresh greens
wait for you
in that field.

196

Welcome,
wild geese —
now you are Japan's.

197

Evening swallow —
no hope for me
tomorrow.

198

Autumn breeze —
fireflies creep off
the verandah.

199

Autumn cicada —
flat on his back,
chirps his last song.

200

Eating alone —
how wild
the autumn wind.

201

Autumn rain,
reflects light
on cramped knees.

202

Good world —
grass field swollen
with dumplings.

203

Autumn eve —
gifting my lap,
paulownia leaf.

204

Mare sucks air —
her foal laps
at the spring.

205

Dawn — fog
of Mt. Asama spreads
on my table.

206

My old home —
wherever I touch,
thorns.

207

Stone Buddha —
whose flower
does he hold?

208

My limbs sharp
as iron nails,
in autumn wind.

209

High and higher,
loveliest of kites —
from the beggar's hut.

210

Autumn dusk —
learning to write
in the blue sky.

211

Kite folded
in arms,
he dreamt on.

212

Autumn morning —
sky's fever,
gone.

213

Strong wind —
mother, suckling child
sheltered by scarecrow.

214

Autumn wind —
scarlet flowers my child
might well have picked.

215

Young horse
leaving its birthplace,
in autumn rain.

216

Giant of a man,
homeless
in autumn wind.

217

Evening — above
kitchen smoke and my
poor knees, wild geese!

218

Child,
trying to pluck
dew-pearls.

219

High on the hill,
I cough
into the autumn gust.

220

Shifting the babe on
her back, vendor cries,
"Sardines" to barley reapers.

221

Autumn wind — compass
points out my
old mountain home.

222

Woodpecker on
the temple pillar —
die! die! die!

223

Cool breeze —
two helpings
scarcely satisfy.

224

Clouds burst
from rice paddies,
day and night.

225

Snails deserting
shells,
in autumn wind.

226

My thinning hair,
eulalia grass,
rustling together.

227

Chrysanthemum —
hidden from man, how
straight you'd grow.

228

Autumn cold —
night after night,
death-chant of earthworms.

229

Tortoise scrimping
in the pond — when
will you eat again?

230

"How am I doing?"
Sponge cucumber
hanging on cactus.

231

Weeds —
lengthen
with the days.

232

Rope of fog
snaring
the hedge.

233

Autumn night
whistles —
a rip in the *shoji*.

234

Tucked under
a paulownia leaf —
sleeping dog.

235

Waiting the eclipse —
where have
the moonstruck fled?

236

Stillness —
clouds peak
in the lake.

237

Mountain cuckoo —
spirit
of the forest.

238

Autumn wind —
once, it too
was fresh.

239

Splash —
crow into
white dew.

240

Passing wild geese,
lighting night
mountains of Shinano.

241

By lightning,
I creak
across the bridge.

242

Foggy night —
splash, here I am
in the pool.

243

Autumn freeze —
wherever I turn up,
I'm sponger.

244

Autumn mountain —
"We're still alive up here,"
boom temple gongs.

245

Horse-bean flowers
again — time
to change our clothes.

246

Mid-October —
tea ceremony
ten days long!

247

Eulalia grass —
more withered,
the louder.

248

Surrounding
my old home, knives
of eulalia grass.

249

Bright moon,
welcome to my hut —
such as it is.

250

Autumn wind — I'm
coming closer to the age
of grandma's death.

251

Puppy —
leaping for
the kite-tail.

252

Snake on the sacred
mountain —
world sloughed off,

253

Slanders — lost
behind
fortune's white wall.

254

Here, in autumn
of my life,
a perfect moon.

255

Evening rain,
nest burnt-out:
the pheasant's face.

256

Paulownia tree —
as leaves whiz down,
how proud you stand.

257

Autumn butterfly,
clinging
to scarecrow's sleeve.

258

Autumn wind —
cock's crowing
on the rooftop.

259

Wild geese, homing
once more through smoke
of Mt. Asama.

260

Over the town,
kites lined
in sunset.

261

Haze swirling
the gate —
who comes?

262

Harvesting barley —
even corner-stones
drip with sweat.

263

Autumn evening —
left behind
once more, by others.

264

Autumn mountains,
surrendering
to dusk.

265

Morning rain —
the usual plunge
of a paulownia leaf.

266

Evening temple gong —
woodpecker
stops, listens.

267

Autumn evening —
over clasped knees
the monk's rapt face.

268

Tonight you too
are rushed,
autumn moon.

WINTER

269

Just by being,
I'm here —
in snow-fall.

270

Over paddies
at its foot,
smoke of Mt. Asama.

271

Changing clothes,
but not
the wanderer's lice.

272

Lost in bamboo,
but when moon lights —
my house.

273

One bath
after another —
how stupid.

274

Winter lull —
no talents,
thus no sins.

275

Kites shriek
together —
departure of the gods.

276

About the field
crow moves
as if he's tilling.

277

Outliving
them all, all —
how cold.

278

Worldly sky —
from now on
every year's a bonus.

279

Closer, closer
to paradise —
how cold.

280

Cool breeze,
twisting, winding —
here at last.

281

Even in warmest
glow, how
cold my shadow.

282

Over fading
eulalia,
cold's white ghost.

283

Sky of Shinano —
no joke,
all this snow.

284

Snowy field —
now rice is down,
more geese than men.

285

Hazy afternoon
in the temple hall —
never such calm.

286

By light from
the next room, I freeze
at the inn table.

287

Sixty years —
not one night
have I danced.

288

New Year — cast out,
house on fire,
nestless birds and I.

289

My village
traced through haze —
still an eyesore.

290

Lovely — galaxy
through torn screen
near my sickbed.

291

Year's end fair —
"What d'*you* want here?"
they ask me.

292

Year's frantic close —
how calm
night sky.

293

Snug under quilt,
spot drenched
Daimyo passing.

294

Silverfish escaping —
mothers,
fathers, children.

295

Sprawled like an X —
how carefree,
how lonely.

296

Melting snow —
the village flows
with children.

297

Winter's here —
around the fire,
stench of gossip.

298

Telescope —
eyeful of haze,
three pence.

299

"Gray starling!"
they sneer behind me,
freezing the bone.

300

At the fireside,
smiling
his last farewell.

301

Leaning against
the pillar —
how cold the blood.

302

Winter rain —
at dusk the horse, too,
neighs for home.

303

Far over the
withered field,
light from a hut.

304

Hazy evening —
in the hill's shadow,
flute of the candy-man.

305

Twilight mist —
horse remembers the gap
in the bridge.

306

Gathering mist,
eternal mornings —
how good the tea.

307

Evenings, all I
can do is stroke
my ribs — such cold.

308

Ambrosial snow,
softly, whitely,
flake on flake.

309

Winter wind —
squatting street singer
serenades dusk-shadows.

310

Through snow
a "For Rent" sign,
not there yesterday.

311

Winter wind —
a salt-fish
wrapped in oak bark.

312

Hut in mist —
is the owner married, then,
or free?

313

Showering
onto Mt. Kiso,
the Milky Way.

314

Chilly night —
horse neighing,
"Here's the outhouse!"

315

Haloed
by snowflakes —
lovely moon.

316

Youth gone —
brushwood hardly splits
across the knee.

317

Through biting winter
rain, smoke
of baking clams.

318

Bare-legged
under cold moon —
Gods of old.

319

New Year's Day —
up there,
never such blue.

320

Winter moon —
outer moat
cracks with cold.

321

Cockscombs blasted
by winter sleet —
such vengeance!

322

Cloud on cloud
stream down
into the lake.

323

Snowy path —
dogs
clear the way.

324

What a moon —
if only she were here,
my bitter wife.

325

Year's end —
blue sky beckons
to Moriya.

326

Buried in snow
well into spring —
my village.

327

Charcoal fire —
spark by spark,
we fade too.

328

Hailstones —
tumbling
into the fire.

329

Winter nights deepening —
henceforth
creaking pillars.

330

Crow in willow —
as if
nothing happened.

331

How cool —
cloud lofted
like a handball.

332

New Year's Day —
blizzard of
plum blossoms.

333

My parents' home —
was moon
ever so bright?

334

Still meadow horse —
monument
of snow.

335

Temple gong frozen —
this side of the mountain
I shiver in bed.

336

Dozing, waking,
yawning —
cat's on for love.

337

Year's end —
who drinks not,
gains not.

338

Pine-wreath and I
listen to rain
this New Year's Eve.

339

Where in the galaxy
does it wait,
my wandering star?

340

First snow on
the village, through
a crack in the wall.

341

Melting snow —
how very
round the moon!

342

Such rousers —
only daylight will
curb their song.

343

Cold night —
weasel tricks
the shrine priest.

344

Strong wind —
dog drags
two samurai.

345

Moonlit wall —
frozen shadow
of the pine.

346

Botching my rest,
winter storming
the floor-boards.

347

Through blinding snow
light quivers from
the smallpox hut.

348

Milky Way — windbags
in the capital
struck dumb by you.

349

Driftwood
to and fro —
year's end.

350

Winter storms
the empty
manger wall.

351

Stubble fields
around my hut,
I'm famished!

352

After long away,
I found
a clouded moon.

353

Winter fields —
garden sparrows
begging rice.

354

Poor winter village —
frosted on notice-board:
"No charity."

355

Winter-night plovers —
not
one old voice.

356

Moonlight babblers —
drunk
and stone-deaf chum.

357

Temple swept,
vermilion candles
warm the altar-hall.

358

Poor snow —
clinging
to that rough wall.

359

Crowned with snow,
cow staggers
under its load.

360

Fresh start —
New Year's dinner,
on my own.

361

Faint, over the moonlit
slope, a frozen
temple gong.

362

Snowy night —
who passes
so silent?

363

Light haze —
his sedge hat
waving goodbye.

364

Winter rain:
who does Stone Buddha
wait for?

365

Hush crickets —
here's first
winter rain.

366

World of dew?
Perhaps,
and yet . . . .

NOTES

1. Issa was among the first haiku poets to insist, at times ironically, that beauty can be found in anything.

10. Buddhism's highest achievement, the attainment of Nirvana, cannot be gained through ritual alone, nor of course can it be bought through donations.

11. The plum is the first fruit tree to bloom in Japan, in the south as early as February.

21. In cherry-blossom season many gather for parties under the trees.

22. Mokuboji, a Buddhist temple often visited by the poet.

26. The ducks which have survived the hunting season.

27. Scorched rocks at the foot of Mt. Asama, the volcano.

29. Issa's house was burnt down in Kashiwabara's great fire in 1827.

35. Among poets, one of Issa's most admired pieces.

44. In this, one of his most celebrated poems, Issa is — as so often — talking to himself.

45. The cormorant is being scolded by the fisherman. Cormorants are leashed together with rings around their throats (hence they cannot swallow their catch) in cormorant-fishing.

46. In the sense of "all ours," nature being common property.

54. Hakone, a very difficult pass near Atami, was dared by the poet in 1792, at the age of 29.

60. "Coop-birds" confined for fattening.

83. A chipped cup suggests Issa's life-long poverty.

89. Japan's heat and humidity assure a plenitude of mosquitoes.

90. Prayer-beads are used by Buddhists.

92. Japanese cats are expert cicada-trackers.

97. The Japanese striped melon resembles a leopard-frog.

99. Written on a walking tour in Shimofusa.

100. The purpose of the annual Buddhist Bon Festival, July 13-15, is to perpetuate the memory of ancestors.

105. Written in 1819 and related to his daughter Sato's death, as described in *Oraga Haru.*

106. Issa's note on this piece, 1821, reveals that it was written seventeen days after his second son's death.

109. Written while crossing Hakone Pass, at a time when the poet was living as a Buddhist monk.

115. Issa's poor kitchen, at dawn.

117. Flower-field (*hano-no* in romanized Japanese) is in haiku a "season word." Autumn is approaching.

119. Written in 1819: Issa saw in dream his dead daughter Sato's face.

120. In Issa's snow country there is sudden thawing in early summer, making it ideal for mosquitoes. Yet the old look forward to the warmth.

122. Fukagawa, an oyster town on the Sumida River.

127. Mating season for cats.

149. Written in 1795, at Dogo Hot Springs.

150. Adapted from a poem in the Chinese classic *Shikyo (Book of Songs)* which Issa read with deep interest all his life.

159. Written in 1811, after a farmer's field had been confiscated to make room for a new manor.

160. The bean-curd man, calling his wares, would appear at around noon.

163. The priest's life, journeying from one temple to another.

166. The symbolic weight of such a poem would not have been lost on the poet's readers.

170. The leaves of the banana plant are very large.

173. It was customary, in the cool of summer evening, to sprinkle the paths and dash water over tethered horses.

176. The piece is a parody on a poem in the earliest collection of Japanese verse, the eighth-century *Manyoshu*.

179. *Dharma*, or Buddhist Law, is manifested in all living things.

185. The poem is all the more interesting because the poet's pen-name is colloquial for a cup of tea. The irony: one could purchase a nightingale or drink a cup of tea for the smallest of sums.

187. No flower is more greatly prized in Japan than the ever-present morning-glory.

190. Dense smudge was used to keep off mosquitoes. Mosquito netting has been used for centuries in Japan.

192. *Futon*, or bedding, are always aired.

196. Wild geese migrate to Japan from Siberia. When they reach Sotogahana, at the country's northern tip, they are welcomed back.

202. The field grasses will soon be turned into dumplings.

208. In 1813 the poet returned, ill, after three months on the road.

214. Written after his daughter Sato's death in 1819.

217. At the age of 47, the poet was beginning to feel his age: "my poor knees." He could not, in other words, leap up to see the wild geese.

223. Composed in 1822. Kiku, the poet's wife, had just recovered from gout, and was hungry.

225. The point is that though snails do not "desert" their shells, the wind is strong enough to tear them from them.

228. Though they have no vocal organs, earthworms often sing in haiku.

229. A Tokyo poem, for Issa notes he writes of Shinobazu Pond.

235. A poem done in 1819. Issa's note: "total eclipse of the moon."

244. In 1795 the poet visited Saimyoji Temple to see Charai, the head priest, who had died, he discovered, some time before. He was wandering from place to place.

245. The common broad-bean.

250. Written in 1808. Issa's note: "the thirty-third anniversary of grandma's death."

253. The white wall (*shirakabe*) symbolizes great wealth, thus is often spoken ill of by the envious.

254. Composed three years before the poet's death.

262. Everyone sweats when barley is harvested.

263. Written in 1806, when the poet and an eighty-year-old companion were returning together from a temple. He could hardly keep up with him. The poem's symbolic intention is clear.

266. Not only the temple, but the gong, were of wood.

267. The monk had the look of one who had experienced enlightenment.

270. Mt. Asama, northwest of Karuizawa on the boundary between Nagano and Gumma prefectures, is along with Mt. Aso in Kyushu one of the most active volcanoes in Japan.

271. Issa was as much a wanderer as his favorite poet, Basho.

275. Though gods have their place in Japanese mythology and Buddhist literature, Issa as devoted Buddhist would not have been believed in a Supreme Being.

277. Issa's first wife and their children died before him.

279. In a sense, though it was not referred to as such, Issa's "death poem."

283. Shinano (now Nagano) Prefecture, where the poet was born, has heavy snowfall.

286. The next room at the inn, having good light, was superior to his. The light shone through the paper wall.

287. On this sober piece W. B. Yeats based an exuberant short poem, "Imitated from the Japanese," which in part goes:
      A most astonishing thing—
      Seventy years have I lived . . .
      And never have I danced for joy.

297. There is much time, around the fire in winter, for gossip.

298. A peek through the telescope at a teahouse near Yushima Shrine cost three pence.

316. Written in 1817, at the age of 54.

317. Composed in the old castle town Kuwana, famous for baked clams.

321. Good example of Issa's taste for personification, with winter sleet pictured as avenger — the hardy cockscombs have not yet fallen.

324. Composed in autumn of 1823, the year of Kiku's death.

325. In 1810 the poet left Tokyo to greet the New Year at the Sairiuji Temple in Moriya, where his fellow poet Kakuro lived. This is the first piece of a *renga* (linked haiku composed jointly by two or more poets), done with Kakuro.

329. The poem gives a sense of Issa's lowered spirits, in hard times: in August 1824 he divorced his second wife Yuki, and had another attack of palsy.

332. Kashiwabara is in blizzard country.

333. The poet's note: "after forty years of wandering."

337. A Japanese saying: "teetotalers never make millionaires."

338. Written in 1802, first New Year's Day after his father's death. Pine-wreaths decorated the house.

346. Issa's note: "staying at a mountain temple."

347. "Smallpox hut" would have been quarantined.

348. Shinano slang (*ukke*) for windbag or simpleton, one of many such words the poet would bring into his poems.

352. In 1807 the poet returned home after long absence.

353. Issa's note: "the garden of Seibi's former dwelling."

354. Composed in 1818, with the note: "drought-stricken village."

357. As in western churches, candles are burned in Buddhist temples.

360. Composed in 1824. Six years before, Issa celebrated the New Year with his dead wife Kiku and their daughter Sato, whose death is lamented in *Oraga Haru*.

BOOKS BY LUCIEN STRYK

Taproot
The Trespasser
Zen: Poems, Prayers, Sermons, Anecdotes, Interviews
Notes for a Guidebook
Heartland: Poets of the Midwest
World of the Buddha: An Introduction to Buddhist Literature
The Pit and Other Poems
Afterimages: Zen Poems of Shinkichi Takahashi
Twelve Death Poems of the Chinese Zen Masters
Zen Poems of China and Japan: The Crane's Bill
Awakening
Heartland II: Poets of the Midwest
Three Zen Poems
Selected Poems
Haiku of the Japanese Masters
The Duckweed Way: Haiku of Issa
The Penguin Book of Zen Poetry
The Duckpond
Prairie Voices: Poets of Illinois
Zen Poems
Encounter with Zen: Writings on Poetry and Zen
Cherries
Bird of Time: Haiku of Basho
Willows
Collected Poems 1953–1983
On Love and Barley: Haiku of Basho
Triumph of the Sparrow: Zen Poems of Shinkichi Takahashi
Bells of Lombardy
Of Pen and Ink and Paper Scraps
The Dumpling Field: Haiku of Issa

A NOTE ABOUT THE AUTHOR AND TRANSLATORS

Kobayashi Issa (1763–1827) has long been considered, with Basho, Buson, and Shiki, one of Japan's greatest haiku poets. He was born in Kashiwabara in the province of Shinano (now Nagano Prefecture), and though he spent much time away from his native place, in Tokyo and on long journeys throughout the country, his emotional and creative life was centered there. Many of his poems are filled with compassion for the life of creatures, and all seem inspired by Buddhist faith. No poet of Japan is more greatly loved.

Lucien Stryk's most recent collections are *Collected Poems 1953–1983* (1984), *On Love and Barley: Haiku of Basho* 1985), *Bells of Lombardy (1986)* and *Of Pen and Ink and Paper Scraps* 1989. He has brought out a book of essays. *Encounters with Zen,* and is editor of *World of the Buddha: An Introduction to Buddhist Literature.* With the late Takashi Ikemoto he translated *Zen Poems of China and Japan, Triumph of the Sparrow: Zen Poems of Shinkichi Takahashi* and *The Penguin Book of Zen Poetry,* which received the Islands and Continents Translation Award and the Society of Midland Authors Poetry Award. He has held a Fulbright grant and two visiting lectureships in Japan, and presently holds a research professorship, teaching Asian literature, creative writing and poetry, at Northern Illinois University.

Noboru Fujiwara, who died in 1989, lived in Toyonaka, a suburb of Osaka. A retired university lecturer, he was a leading member of the Tenro School of Haiku, one of the most distinguished in Japan. Inspired by haiku's "great four," his own haiku are known to many who care for the art throughout the country.